CRISSCROSS
APPLESAUCE
AND SHUT THE HELL UP

CRISSCROSS APPLESAUCE
AND SHUT THE HELL UP

10 Reflective Lessons for New and Seasoned Teachers

Colleen Schmit

FOUR
monkeys press

Omaha, Nebraska

CRISSCROSS APPLESAUCE AND SHUT THE HELL UP
10 REFLECTIVE LESSONS FOR NEW AND SEASONED TEACHERS

Four Monkeys Press books are available from your favorite bookseller or from www.FourMonkeysPress.com

Four Monkeys Press
c/o CMI
13518 L Street
Omaha, NE 68137

ISBN: 978-0-9973508-1-4 (sc)
ISBN: 978-0-9973508-2-1 (Mobi)
ISBN: 978-0-9973508-3-8 (EPUB)

Library of Congress Cataloging Number 2016934508
Cataloging in Publication data on file with the publisher.

Printed in the USA

10 9 8 7 6 5 4 3 2

This book is dedicated to the hundreds of students, parents, and educators of South Omaha who have shaped me as a teacher and influenced me greatly as a person. I am eternally grateful for all of my varied learning experiences in the classroom.

I also dedicate this book to my beautiful children, Kaitlyn, Scarlett, Will, and "new baby." Becoming a mother inspired me to think about the educational experiences they may have and how I could possibly impact this by positively influencing teachers.

CONTENTS

I knew I wanted to be a teacher from a young age. It's something I have always known. I never felt the struggle that some feel at eighteen, when you have to decide what to be when you grow up. I just knew; I could feel it in my bones. Teaching young children is what I was meant to do.

After graduation I was hired as a kindergarten teacher and taught for eight years at a public school with a very demanding student population. Eighty-five percent of the students qualified for free/reduced lunch;

there was a thirty-three percent mobility rate; and eighty-eight percent of the children were classified as English Language Learners. I loved my job, but somewhere along the road, I felt I lost my way. My passion never died, but I started to become crotchety! You know the type— teachers that complain about everything. I'm sure everyone has encountered one or more of these teachers in their academic journey, and I was quickly becoming one. I was annoyed with my colleagues, frustrated with the demands of the district, and I felt that I knew better than any training I would ever be forced to attend.

How could this have happened? When I began my career I was "Little Miss Susie Sunshine." Teaching was exhausting, but I felt good about what I was doing. I could laugh with my students. It didn't matter if the kids weren't sitting crisscross applesauce and listening with perfect attention like little soldiers. I didn't care about that. We were having fun! Center time was long and meaningful. My students were able to discover with blocks, learn through painting, and explore through dramatic play in the house center. I tied in our thematic units to our learning centers to increase social studies and science exposure. Lots of great hands-on experiences were happening. We were learning to love learning.

As a new teacher, the expectations of other educators can gradually sway the way you run your classroom. You feel like you are doing the school a disservice if you have students who sit on their knees to listen on the carpet or don't raise their hands when sharing an answer. Center time is seen as a waste of instructional time. How silly is that? When did educators start adopting the attitude that children aren't learning while playing? That concept goes against every Early Childhood core education class I've ever taken in both undergrad and grad school.

But alas, I began to conform to the herd. My students soon became little soldiers adhering to classroom expectations that really weren't helping to serve learning. I began teaching in a dual-language classroom, and the poor kids were lucky to receive twenty minutes of center time a day, not to mention only fifteen minutes allocated for recess. Sheesh! I spent the bulk of my instructional time reminding my students of our classroom expectations, ensuring that everyone was "giving me five" at all times, and dominating the classroom with teacher talk.

I began to not have fun with teaching. With a regime like that, who would enjoy it? I still loved my students, but it wasn't the same as in my early years. Somewhere along the line, I had changed my teaching style to conform, and because of this, I was looked upon as a model teacher by administrators. My evaluations were always impeccable, but reflecting upon this makes me question what I was really being evaluated on—classroom expectations and the ability to write up a stellar lesson plan following the district format. I know I wasn't being evaluated on the types of relationships I was forming with my students or how they were learning through play. The lesson plans I wrote to follow the district format did not reflect what I was implementing in my classroom during my best teaching moments.

Finally, after my eighth year of teaching, I had had enough. I was burned out and frustrated. I knew I needed to take a break from teaching before I lost myself and became a crusty, old schoolmarm. I had also just had my second child and was finding it difficult to meet the needs of my children at home and my children at school. Working in a high-needs school required special attention and extra work, but so did being a new mother of two. I felt that I was always sacrificing somewhere, and I didn't like how that made me behave at school or at home.

A fellow teaching friend referred me to a job as a program evaluator at the University of Nebraska Medical Center. I was thrilled! I would still be working in the field of education, but I could take a break from being an actual classroom teacher. Perfecto! It also enabled me to work a flexible schedule that allowed for more time at home with my own precious babies.

Part of my new job as an evaluator was to observe teachers using various observational tools and meet with the teachers to go over the scores as determined by the tool. It was like I had been hit upside the head with a two by four. Observing other teachers while learning new and enlightening observational methods made me reflect on my time as an educator.

I realized that a lot of what I was doing as a first-year teacher should have carried on throughout my career. Of course! I should have allowed more opportunities for students to take the lead in their learning. Student talk and peer conversations should have been a major part of my classroom, just like they were in my first years of teaching. Why is this so hard for us as educators? Many will blame the demands of testing and assessment, which I agree plays a role, but as educators, I think we need to take some accountability for our actions. The assessments weren't forcing me to be a drill sergeant to five-year-olds.

I had lost sight of what really mattered, and I strongly believe that taking a break from teaching these last few years is going to make me a significantly better teacher when I'm ready to go back. It also gave me time to be introspective and reflect on my teaching journey, which inspired me to write this book. I want to speak to first-year and pre-service teachers to give insight on mistakes I've made, lessons I've learned, and how to keep the joy alive in teaching. I also want to inspire seasoned teachers to take a breath. It's important to make time in your busy schedule to reflect upon what you are doing in the classroom and if you are meeting your students' needs the best you can.

The following objectives are written in a lesson plan format. My hope is that you are able to refer back to these lessons when you feel like you are losing at teaching. I know I felt that way often, particularly later in my career. I wish I would have kept true to my rookie self and enjoyed the teaching experience more the first time around!

OBJECTIVE 1

Educator will roll with the punches.

Anticipatory Set:

Rocking the '70s Blocks

I was hired for my first teaching job in September. The kids had already begun their school year in August. This meant I would be taking half of the students from a fellow kindergarten teacher who had children coming out of his ears. The school had switched from half-day to full-day kindergarten, but had not allocated for the need of an actual extra teacher. I was thrilled to be hired! It did not matter where or what I was teaching; I was just excited to have an actual teaching job.

I was called in for my interview to meet the principal and see the school. I was told the school was being remodeled, so we would begin the year in a warehouse that had been converted into classrooms. Great! I didn't care. I showed up for my interview with my student teaching portfolio and dressed in my best JC Penney's suit that my dad had bought me as a graduation gift. I was ready to answer all of the questions the principal would ask me. I reviewed interviewing strategies, updated my teaching portfolio, and made sure my résumé listing my employment at Pier 1 Imports and daycare centers was up to date. I was nervous and excited all at the same time.

When I arrived at the school/warehouse I was not ready for what I saw. These were not classrooms! They were big cubicles. How was I supposed to teach in that? And it was loud! You could hear the content of every lesson of each classroom when you walked down the hall. My expectation was to at least have walls in my classroom. *Hmmm, okay...* I thought. *Maybe this really isn't going to be like the teaching experience I had planned in my head.* My interview that I had stayed up half of the night worrying about consisted of two questions—"Do you like small children?" and "When can you start?"

Upon arriving at my new job, I basically had nothing with me. I had purchased an oversized calendar and a multicolored alphabet banner at the local teacher supply shop. I figured the school would provide everything else I needed. Nope. I walked into my classroom made of partitions and all that was supplied was a box of wooden blocks that I am certain had been around since 1972. *Oh, poop! This would not do. How in the world am I supposed to teach with no toys or manipulatives?* I thought to myself. *I should have done a better job of asking questions at my nonexistent interview! Can I change my mind?* I really thought my new classroom would look like the rooms from the videos I watched in teachers college. Where was my cozy rocking chair for reading and my colorful rugs?!

Having only the '70s blocks in my classroom was actually the best thing to happen to me as a new teacher. I had the advantage of knowing exactly what was in my classroom. I did not inherit a bunch of old photocopies and junk from a previous teacher who had acquired thirty years of stuff. My colleagues were more than happy to share counting bears, kitchen toys, and lots of other goodies. Not having much forced me to be more creative in how I implemented lessons. Soon my classroom was stocked with everything we needed. The kiddos took good care of what we had in the room (mainly, I think, because there wasn't that much of it). The thoughts I had of what my classroom "should be" did not meet my expectations, but everything did turn out to be more than all right.

Procedure:

1. This one is simple. One step. Go with the flow. You may not be assigned to the grade you imagined, placed at the school you wanted, or have the classroom you envisioned. Try to stay positive and make the best of it. Complaining and lamenting over the situation will only make you miserable. Look for the good in the experience and see it as part of your journey as a teacher.

Closing:

My first year I quickly learned that in education you have to be able to roll with the punches. Not everything is going to be just as you imagined it. Try to keep a positive attitude when things are not going your way. Being negative will only drag you down. Letting go of your own ideal teaching world and embracing challenge and change will be key to maintaining your sanity as a new teacher.

Reflection Questions:

1. What were some of your expectations as a first-year teacher?

2. How did you handle going with the flow when things didn't go as planned?

3. What strategies have you learned to better react to roadblocks that you may encounter in education?

"The only way to make sense out of change is to plunge into it, move with it, and join the dance."

—Alan W. Watts

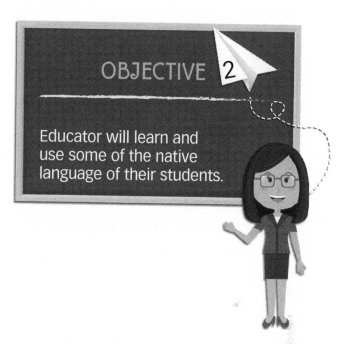

OBJECTIVE 2

Educator will learn and use some of the native language of their students.

Anticipatory Set:

"¡Hola chola!"

My first year of teaching was a learning year to say the least. Our school was being renovated, and we were relocated to a large building that was big enough to allow for multiple schools to occupy it at the same time while updates were made at the home school. The classrooms were divided by partitions and sound was an issue. You could hear what was happening in all of the classrooms surrounding your room.

As I mentioned earlier, the school I was assigned to had eighty-eight percent English Language Learners. The majority of the students at the school were Spanish speakers or had Spanish spoken in their homes. I had taken Spanish in high school and for a year in college, but was far from being fluent. Many of my students that year entered kindergarten without being able to speak a word of English. This seemed like a daunting task to my fresh-out-of-college self. I was terrified. How in the world was I going to teach these kiddos everything they needed to learn in kindergarten when they didn't even understand the words coming out of my mouth? As an optimistic newbie, I decided this would be the perfect opportunity for us to learn a new language together. I could learn to speak more Spanish and hopefully help my students to learn English.

And learn I did. One fall morning, I was walking down the hall towards the restroom with my line of students following me like little ducks. Both times we passed a certain classroom of one of the other schools sharing a space in the building, a little boy in my class named Juan hollered out, "¡Hola chola!" and waved at the teacher inside the room, Ms. Jackson. He then looked at me, beaming, and said, "The chola lives there. That's the chola." Ms. Jackson had no clue who he was, but she smiled and waved back at Juan. I had no idea what he meant by, "Hola chola." This happened every day, twice a day, for a few weeks.

This exchange always seemed pleasant, so I never questioned Juan's intent. I asked a teacher's aide in another kindergarten classroom what the Spanish word "chola" meant. "Oh. I think he is telling her she's beautiful. Chola means beautiful." Mind you, this teacher's aide was not a native Spanish speaker, but her skills were incredibly better than mine, so I trusted her with her definition. The dance with Juan and Ms. Jackson went on. Every time we walked by her room he would shout, "¡Hola chola!" They would wave and smile at each other. I began adding to the situation by praising Juan for using such nice words and being a very friendly boy. "Oh, Juan. That is just so kind! You are such a nice boy," I would say. "He says you're beautiful, Ms. Jackson. Isn't he sweet?"

One day during our typical bathroom break encounter, Mrs. Lopez, a native Spanish-speaking teacher's aide, heard the exchange. Upon hearing Juan call another teacher a chola, she proceeded to get down in Juan's face and speak very quickly and sternly at him in Spanish. "What? What happened? He is just telling her how he thinks she's beautiful!" I quickly intervened. Mrs. Lopez looked at me as if I was the biggest dumb-dumb on the block. "No, mija. He is calling her a gangster. Chola means gangster in Spanish." Oh. Um. Hmm. I had just been encouraging a five-year-old to call another adult a gangster. Major first-year teacher fail.

I decided to let Ms. Jackson continue to think that chola meant beautiful and quickly found a new route for our class to take to the restrooms. I also decided then and there that five-year-olds are sneaky by nature. I vowed to learn enough Spanish that this type of situation couldn't easily happen again.

Slowly, I started to learn more Spanish. I asked native speakers at my school for their help, made attempts to communicate with parents in Spanish, and had help from the best teachers of all—the kindergartners. Eventually, I became a Spanish dual-language teacher and taught all of my lessons only in Spanish with the help of a wonderful teacher's aide from Argentina.

Making the decision to learn the language of my students impacted my interactions with them greatly. It definitely helped to build a sense of team and emphasized that we were on the journey together. *I will learn a new language too! Just like you.* It made me more relatable, not only to them, but to their parents as well.

There were A LOT of learning errors on my part (I still say ridiculous things in Spanish); however, I am forever grateful to my five-year-old teachers and their parents. Honestly, if you want to learn a new language, young children are the best teachers. If I am speaking with a Spanish-speaking adult and make a mistake with conjugating a verb or if I pronounce something wrong, adults say nothing. They feel like correcting me is rude. Kindergartners do not follow this same rule. They will immediately call you out and correct your error. In my experience, learning through mistakes is the best way to learn.

Procedures:

1. Find books that are at the beginner level for the language that you are wanting to learn. I found it very helpful to read leveled-A books in Spanish to learn basic vocabulary. If you can, read these books to your students when you have a few minutes to spare. It's so fun to see your students perk right up when you read something that is in their native language. The English-speaking kiddos get a kick out of books in a different language too! So it's a win-win for all.

2. Write down and USE basic phrases with the families of your students, particularly during drop off or pick up times. They truly do appreciate you trying. Don't be afraid that you are saying something wrong. They probably won't correct your mistake, but by attempting to speak their language, you are helping to build meaningful relationships with the family.

3. Take a class at a community college or consider purchasing a computer program designed to teach language (i.e. Rosetta Stone® or DuoLingo.com). Often times, principals or administrators may have funds available to help you learn a new language, especially if that language is dominant throughout the school.

4. Find a mentor or friend who you feel comfortable practicing with. Using the language is really the only way that you are going to learn it. Don't be afraid or embarrassed to use what you are learning.

5. Practice with your students. Remember how I mentioned they are the best teachers? It's true! When I was learning Spanish, the kids loved to help me learn new phrases and thought my mistakes were hilarious. They had no problem whatsoever correcting me.

Closing:

There are many educators who work in schools where the majority of students speak a language other than English, and they never make an attempt to learn the native language of their students. They feel that it is too hard or they don't have the time to spend learning a new language. I am here to tell you that is not the case. It is worth the effort to attempt to learn the language your students speak. I do realize that Spanish is a very common language and easily accessible. Some languages may be harder to find materials for or find mentors to practice with. We are lucky enough to teach in a time where language is easily accessible on the internet. Simply learning a few phrases can help make students and parents feel welcome in the classroom. It proves to the students and their families that you care about their heritage and respect their culture. It is an effective way to build meaningful relationships with your kids. Learning their language can also prevent sneaky student behavior, such as calling other adults gangsters.

Reflection Questions:

1. How do you think learning the language of your students could impact student learning?

2. How could learning your students' native languages impact your relationship with students and their families?

3. What are some small steps you could take in order to learn a new language?

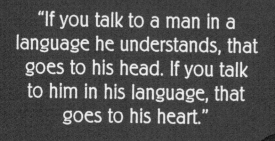

"If you talk to a man in a language he understands, that goes to his head. If you talk to him in his language, that goes to his heart."

–Nelson Mandela

OBJECTIVE 3

Educator will communicate
positively with students
and stand up to bullies.

Anticipatory Set:

Be Nice and Have Fun

Something sad is happening in our schools. It doesn't matter what city you teach in or what type of population the school is serving. A LOT of teachers have lost the ability to smile and have fun with their students. A negative teaching climate can be found in any school you enter at any time of the year. It doesn't matter what age level you observe. This is not only an upper elementary or secondary problem—it is happening in Early Childhood classrooms across the board. Yelling, humiliating, and just plain being mean is everywhere. The worst part is that this type of behavior has become an accepted norm by educators and administrators alike.

When I was teaching, if I saw a colleague berating or screaming at a student in the hall, I would turn a blind eye. It made me uncomfortable, but not enough to do something about it. That is because, unfortunately, that type of negativity was not abnormal. That's a scary thought that is worth repeating; teachers screaming at children in school is not abnormal. As a parent of small children, it makes me sick to know that my own children will often be exposed to this behavior in their educational career. I know I was exposed to teachers likes this as a child, and I'm sure you can vividly remember similar examples from your own childhood—severely negative teachers who frequently resorted to nasty sarcasm and overall seemed unhappy with their career choice.

I think we as teachers are forgetting the huge impact we have on our students' lives. An educator's role is to support, nurture, engage, and inspire students. Nowhere in the job description does it say that you are encouraged to humiliate, chastise, or put down your kids! Many of our students come to us from home lives that would break your heart. There is enough negative climate happening at home that it absolutely does not need to be reciprocated at school. Here comes the cool part—we can change this.

First, if you are engaging in this type of behavior, have the strength to recognize that you need help! Reach out to someone at the school that you trust who can talk to you about this type of behavior, and give you on ideas on how to change it. Interacting with students in these negative ways causes severe harm, not only to the student on the receiving end, but also to the students who are witnessing it. The other impactful—and in my opinion even harder—thing to do is to not tolerate this negative behavior from your peers. It takes a lot of courage to stand up and say, "What you are doing is wrong. Yelling at children in a humiliating or sarcastic manner is hurtful, and it needs to stop. How can I help you?" This may result in the end of a friendship with your coworker, but I really think it's worth it. I am so sick of all the accepted negative behavior in our schools I could scream! We need to change this, and guess what? The amazing thing is that we can.

Procedures:

1. Become an advocate for children. When you witness a negative situation that children are being subjected to, think of yourself as a voice for the voiceless. This is a very brave and hard thing to do. Like I mentioned, I turned a blind eye to this type of behavior. I wish I would have stood up and said, "Stop! This is not okay." Ignoring this type of behavior is just adding to the problem. Now be warned, this will not make you the most popular girl or guy at the party. However, as educators, we need to start addressing this type of behavior. Everyone knows it's going on, but not many seem to be doing anything about it.

2. If you are engaging in screaming, berating, or humiliating students, have the courage and strength to recognize that you need help. Reach

out to a counselor, principal, or trusted peer for ideas on how to get this under control. Be a strong enough teacher to change your undesirable and damaging behavior.

Closing:

The message I am trying to convey here is that we need to take action to ensure that negative behavior does not become the accepted norm in our schools and to prevent that negativity from taking over our classrooms. We need to stop screaming at children and give more hugs. Fewer time-outs and more time for "Tell me about how you're feeling, and why you're feeling that way." Smile. Laugh. Enjoy. Let's start having fun again with teaching! This is a very challenging, yet tremendously rewarding career. Not every moment as a teacher is joyful, but shouldn't the majority of the moments be?

Reflection Questions:

1. How does it make you feel when you see a teacher yelling at or humiliating a student?

2. What can you personally do to stop negative teacher behavior that is happening in your school?

3. If **YOU** are the educator who is behaving negatively towards students, what can you do to stop this behavior? Who do you have in your life that you feel safe enough with to ask for help in guiding you to change **YOUR** behavior?

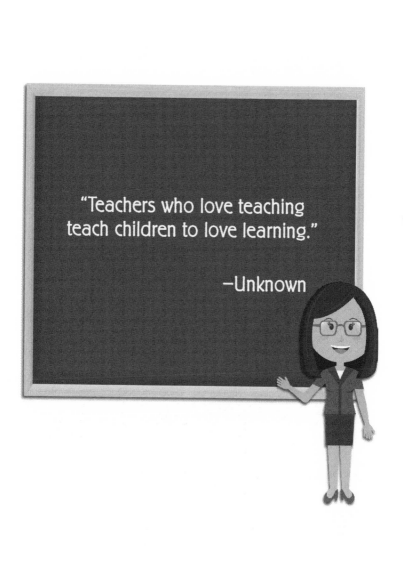

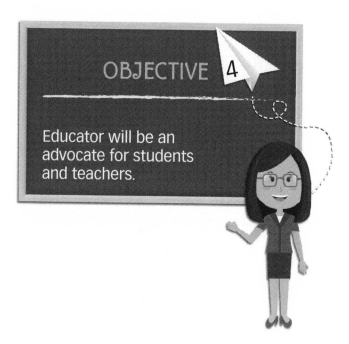

OBJECTIVE 4

Educator will be an advocate for students and teachers.

Anticipatory Set:

Do You Hear the People Sing?

The absence of fun is a disturbing epidemic in many classrooms. Educators have become so wrapped up in the demands posed on them that they are forgetting to enjoy the experience of teaching. The creative spark of educators is quickly fading. When I first began teaching, I smiled and laughed with my students all the time. We sang songs, had long and meaningful center times, and played all sorts of games together. I still did some of those things the last few years that I was a teacher, but it wasn't the same as when I began. I became consumed with making sure we completed all objectives from each day's lesson plan and that I was fitting in all the minutes my district was requiring for each subject area. Testing had become a surprisingly frequent part of my regime. I started teaching in 2003; every year that followed, there were more and more required tests for kindergartners—for five-year-olds! I felt bad for my poor peers who taught third, fourth, fifth, sixth grade, and beyond. The amount of chapter tests, district tests, and state standardized testing these teachers are enduring is sickening.

How policy makers came to the consensus that this is the right thing to do boggles my mind. What in the world are we gaining by doing this to our kids? I know what we are missing out on. I know what these tests aren't showing. These tests don't measure the social and academic gains our students are making every day, how much compassion our students have, their creativity, their self-esteem, their ability to think outside the box, their courage, their kindness, or their grit. The tests don't reflect on you as a teacher either. They can't measure how much you care about your job, how you go the extra mile for your kids, how you have a room where half of the students don't speak the language they are being tested in, or how four of your kids receive special education services, but are still measured by the same silly standardized test. The tests don't show what amazing relationships you are building with those kids and how you spent your entire weekend prepping and differentiating instruction for four different guided-reading and guided-math groups.

I do believe that the tests were originally thought of as helpful tools for measuring learning. I'd like to give policy makers the benefit of the doubt in thinking that by invoking all of this testing they were trying to help our kids. The sad part is, they got it wrong; things need to change, and they need to change now. We can't keep letting this happen in our classrooms. It is killing our creative freedom as educators and stifling student learning. It's an interruption and a nuisance. I didn't sign up to be a teacher to give tests. I signed up to teach.

Aren't we mad enough yet? Can't you hear the lyrics from *Les Misérables* in your head? "Do you hear the people sing? Singing the song of angry men?" Why are we still allowing this high-stakes over-testing to take over our teaching time? The pendulum of education has swung so far over to one side that it has to be ready to swing back. I think all it needs is a little push. A push from us as educators to do something about it. We need to have the strength to say, "ENOUGH! This is not what is best for kids, and we know it."

Procedures:

1. Be an advocate for your students and for yourself as a teacher. Voice your concerns about over-testing to school board members, curriculum specialists, your building principal, and your state representatives and senators.

2. Don't let the silly tests take away your passion for education. Enjoy your students! Be silly, smile, and have fun. Do your best to pump every moment not testing with teachable, meaningful experiences for your kids.

Closing:

The demands coming down from above were stifling who I had set out to be as an educator. I am a person who loves fun and laughing, and I always aspired to incorporate that into my teaching style. Personally, I had hit a point where those things were no longer there in my teaching; I had lost the fun part of my job. Simply put, I was losing my creative spirit as an educator. The demands and curriculum that were constantly pushed down from the district stifled my creative spark and made me not like the way I was teaching. I am not one who can follow a script from a manual. I wanted my students to have a choice in what we were learning about.

The way I was teaching felt unnatural to me, and I knew that in order to be happy and fulfilled in my career, I needed to step away and take some time to regroup. I am a firm believer that when something doesn't feel right, you should STOP doing it. My hope is that by writing this book I can inspire other educators to be more active in standing up for your students and yourself. Let the policy makers know that through over-testing our students, we are ruining our precious time in the classroom to foster learners who are high-level creative thinkers.

Reflection Questions:

1. How are you being an advocate for what you know is best for your students?

2. How are you an advocate for yourself as a teacher?

3. Reflect upon some of your best moments in the classroom. Was testing involved? Why or why not?

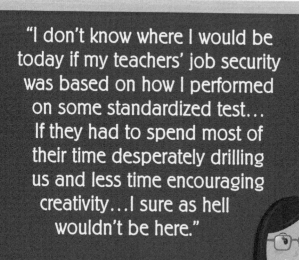

"I don't know where I would be today if my teachers' job security was based on how I performed on some standardized test... If they had to spend most of their time desperately drilling us and less time encouraging creativity...I sure as hell wouldn't be here."

—Matt Damon

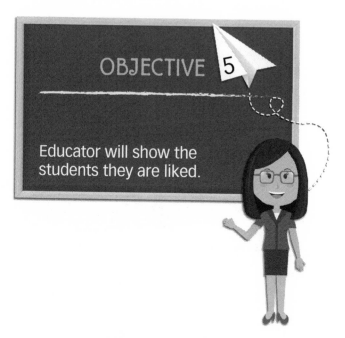

OBJECTIVE 5

Educator will show the students they are liked.

Anticipatory Set:

Getting Kids to Love Learning

Do you want to know the absolute key ingredient to increasing students' scores and outcomes? The answer: getting them to like school! Truly. That is the single greatest thing that a teacher can do to positively affect academic and social/emotional growth in the classroom. If students like you, they will work for you; if they feel safe and secure they will try their best; and, most importantly, if they know you like them and truly care about them, they will strive to make you proud. This is it. This is the key. It's so simple, yet so immensely important.

I always noticed a shift in my relationships with my students after the first parent-teacher conferences in the fall. For the first few years, I couldn't quite figure out why there was such a change. They seemed to work harder, give me more hugs, showcase more of their personalities, and just generally enjoy school more. I always chalked it up to the amount of time they had been in the classroom; maybe it just took twelve weeks for my students to really feel comfortable with me.

I now have a different theory—I think it was the conferences. I really do. I always gave conferences that were strengths-based. During parent/teacher conferences, I told the parents great things about their kids. I showed examples of their work that showcased what they were doing well, and I was not shy about letting the parents know how special I felt their kids were. I discussed with the parents ways to play games at home and emphasized how important spending time reading together was. During my early years, I talked very little about the assessments.

Often times, my students were with their parents at the conferences, so they heard what I said about them. After conferences, my students knew that I liked them. They knew I thought they had strengths and that they were special. I believe this made them feel safe, and in turn, I believe it perhaps made them comfortable enough to show me they liked me too. Remember in your pre-service teacher course work when you learned about Erick Erickson's eight psychosocial development stages? The first stage Erikson emphasized in Childhood and Society was trust versus mistrust with infants and caregivers. When there is a consistent effort to meet a child's needs, he will begin to trust the people caring for him. When these needs are not being met, the child learns to not trust the caregiver.

In my opinion, Erikson's theory about trust versus mistrust applies perfectly to the relationship between you and your students, no different than in Erickson's example about infants and caregivers.

Think about it for a second—if your students are terrified of you, what makes you think that they are going to show you who they really are or what they know? Showing our students through our actions and words that we care about them and fostering an environment and relationship where the students feel safe are the keys to success in the classroom.

Procedures:

1. Compliment your students as a group. Let them know specifically what behaviors or actions they are doing that you would like for them to continue. For example, if I was walking my class down the hall, and they were following the hallway expectations, I would always comment to a passing teacher about my class. "Oh, look, Mr. V. Aren't these kindergartners doing a beautiful job walking quietly in the hall? They are so quiet I forget that they are even behind me." Being specific about praise-worthy behaviors encourages the students to persist with this behavior.

2. Compliment your students as individuals. Try to take the time to have conversations with all of your students each day and fill their buckets with genuine praise. I know making it around to each student every day may be a challenge, but it can have

an extremely positive impact on learning. Another fun way to fill a child's positive bucket is to make a positive phone call home to their parents in front of the child. Both parents and children love this! It's much more frequent that educators call caregivers to share concerns or behavioral issues that when it is a positive phone call home, the impact can be awesome.

3. Consider going on home visits to see where your students live and what environment they come from. Typically this is common practice only in Early Childhood classrooms, but it certainly does not have to be! Home visits can be extremely eye-opening. Ever wonder why a student isn't completing homework or comes to school tired every morning? Many of those issues might stem from their home life. Additionally, home visits give you a platform to build relationships with your students. Taking the time to go on home visits are some of my fondest

moments of teaching. Typically, the teacher coming into the family's home was a BIG deal. The families welcomed me with open arms (and usually food to boot). These visits were so valuable to me because they provided me instant insight into the child's life and allowed me the opportunity to get to know my students and their families on a more personal level.

4. Build relationships with your students that are meaningful. Engage in social conversation. Share facts with your students about your personal life away from school. Ask questions about their interests and hobbies. Be genuine.

Closing:

Get to know your students personally and show them that you like them. Express their strengths in positive notes, compliments, rewards, and praise in front of others. Help them to see you as an adult who cares about them as an individual.

Reflection Questions:

1. How can you genuinely show your students you care for them as individuals?

2. What are some ways you boost class morale in a large group setting?

3. Reflect upon times in your classroom when you shared smiles, laughter, and social conversations with your students. How do you think that positive environment impacted learning?

"They may forget what you said, but they will never forget the way you made them feel."

–Carl W. Buehner

OBJECTIVE 6

Educator will think about walking in parents' shoes.

Anticipatory Set:

Wait in the HALL

The ability to look at things from a caregiver's point of view is an invaluable perspective that I never had until I myself became a parent who had a child entering kindergarten. On the first day of school on my first full year, I allowed parents to come into the classroom when dropping off their babies to me. There were many tears from both parents and students. The parents physically being in the room seemed to make the separation worse for the kids. I was uncomfortable with telling these mamas, "Get going. You're making it harder for everyone!"

I made a decision that, after that year, parents would need to say goodbye to their five-year-olds in the hall and would not be allowed to come into the room during the first week of school. At the time, it seemed to me like this would solve all problems. This strategy worked for the most part. Some kids would cry for ten minutes, but after a bit they would settle down, become acclimated and comfortable in the classroom, and we could continue on with the day. But what my childless-self did not take into consideration was how the parents were coping with this arrangement. Looking back, that was a major omission in my thought process.

Here were these parents—many of whom were new to the United States and did not have positive (or sometimes any) experience with formal schooling—dropping off their babies to a total stranger and leaving them for seven hours. Many of these children had been home with their mothers every day since birth. They had literally never been apart. Now here I was asking them to say a quick goodbye in the hall and leave. My intentions were good; I thought this would make for a smoother transition into school and less of a disruption, but looking back now, I really feel like I whiffed on this one. I wish I would have allowed parents into the room to stay until they were comfortable enough to leave.

I know when my oldest daughter started kindergarten, I was an absolute emotional wreck! I knew the teacher, worked in the district, and taught kindergarten for eight years, but even with all that, I was still a mess. I cannot imagine what the mothers of my students must have been feeling dropping off their children to a woman they didn't know whatsoever and who didn't even really speak the same language as their child. I'm forever grateful for my daughter's kindergarten teacher for allowing me into the room to make sure my child was happy, secure, and ready to begin her school career. Hanging on to those last moments of babyhood is so special for a parent. Starting school is really the first big step into childhood, and that's not easy for parents—especially for eldest children and **particularly** for the moms and dads.

Procedures:

1. With everything you do in the classroom, think of how it would feel if that was the experience your own child was having. How would it feel if you were a parent of a child in your class?

2. Remember that not all parents have had positive experiences in school. You may encounter many parents who have never had a formal education or who have had terrible experiences in or with school. They may be intimidated to enter the classroom and uncomfortable even visiting with you at parent-teacher conferences.

3. Be welcoming to parents. Encourage visitors, plan family days, and make a partnership with parents and/or guardians on educating their children. This does not mean you can't have limits on when visitors are appropriate. I am encouraging you to foster a classroom

where there are multiple opportunities to include parents in the education of their child.

4. Keep communication open on both ends. Make sure families know where they can reach you and that you know at least one way to reach them. Again, I would like to emphasize the importance of making positive phone calls home. Parents are usually shocked and thrilled with this one—particularly the students who have had multiple not-so-great phone calls home in the past. Positive phone calls can set you on a quick path for a meaningful and trusting relationship with parents and students.

Closing:

Becoming a mom made me think about teaching in a different way. However, you do not have to be a parent to think like one. Try to walk in the parents' shoes. Treat every child as if they were your own. Imagine how you would like to be treated if you were a parent of a child in your class. You are with these children for over 1100 hours a year. That's a lot! Think of the influence you have in their lives. Make it count.

Reflection Questions:

1. How do you think parents' past school experiences impact their relationships with you?

2. How would you feel about what is happening in your classroom if you were the parent of a child in your class?

3. How can you help to foster a partnership with your students' parents to become co-teachers in their child's education?

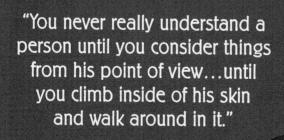

"You never really understand a person until you consider things from his point of view...until you climb inside of his skin and walk around in it."

—Harper Lee

OBJECTIVE 7

Educator will find positive peers to interact with.

Anticipatory Set:

The Mean Girls

When you are a new teacher there are many things that you must navigate. You are bombarded with school procedures and expectations, paperwork, classroom setup, and a million other tasks. One of the very real navigational tasks that no one will warn you about is figuring out the cliques of the school.

It has been my experience that, at every school, there is a little group of mean girls (and/or mean boys) that enjoy spending their time berating others, talking about students and parents, and engaging in other petty junior-high-like behavior.

My best advice for this is to avoid it at all costs. Do not get caught up in the drama. Quite honestly, you shouldn't have the time to even worry about it. Associating with this kind of behavior just adds to the problem. Test the waters in the teacher's lounge as this can be a breeding ground for negativity. If you eat lunch in the lounge for a few days and notice it is a place for educators to be hostile and complain, steer clear! You might find you enjoy eating in your classroom quietly. I tried this and learned that it gave me a chance to regroup and take a breath. Eating in the teacher's lounge and listening to negative comments tended to drain me.

I am NOT suggesting that you isolate yourself; teaching in isolation is a scary thing. You will want to reach out to others.

Look for the experienced teachers who have been teaching for twenty years, but are not counting down to retirement. These teachers have usually figured out how to stay out of the drama and have good insight on what is really important: building positive relationships with students. Avoiding the mean girls and steering clear of unnecessary drama can greatly impact your first few years of teaching. Teaching can be a stressful profession. Why add more stress than is already inevitable?

Procedures:

1. Find a mentor or two. It would be helpful to find someone who teaches the same grade level or subject matter, but that is not essential. What **is** essential is connecting with someone who is positive and wants to help you. You may be assigned a mentor by your school district or principal. If you feel this mentor is not someone who can help you to navigate all the ins and outs of your new job and keep you in a positive place, don't be afraid to seek help elsewhere too.

2. Connect with teachers who LOVE teaching. Positivity breeds positivity. There are countless incredible teachers who love their jobs and can provide great insight on how to have fun while teaching. These people can also be a sounding board when you are feeling upset or need to vent. Just make sure that your new peers don't *only* want to vent.

There are plenty of educators who want nothing more than to find fresh ears to listen to their gripes about the problems within education.

3. Don't be afraid to ask for help, share unique lesson ideas, or connect with others on a personal level. Teaching should not be a competition, but unfortunately it can feel that way all too often. The competitive atmosphere is everywhere—from who has the best test scores to who can design the prettiest bulletin board. This, however, is not what you are there for, so don't get sucked into to this. Share ideas and strategies with your coworkers and they will want to share with you too.

Closing:

It won't take long to figure out who likes to stir up trouble and start drama at a school. With that many people working in a high-stakes, competitive environment, drama is almost assuredly going to show up somewhere in your school. Part of your job is to avoid it and reach out to those who you feel can give you the most positive guidance and support. There are oodles of wonderful educators who have found ways to stay drama-free and focus on their mission of educating children. Stick with these folks and you'll be just fine.

Reflection Questions:

1. In what ways can you collaborate positively with your peers?

2. When and if you encounter school drama while teaching, what can you do to avoid it?

3. Make a list of educators you feel are positive examples of teachers. What qualities do they have that you could learn from to help you to be a better teacher?

"Misery loves good company, so if you are surrounded with drama, gossip, and fools, you may want to consider that you are presently at risk of becoming one of them."

–Bryant McGill

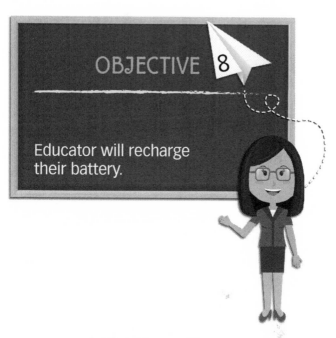

OBJECTIVE 8

Educator will recharge their battery.

Anticipatory Set:

Big Bucks for a Big Price

Around February of my first year, all the teachers in my school received information about teaching summer school. There were two sessions available to teach. Being a twelve-month employee meant you would be paid extra cashola in addition to your regular salary. Whoa! This meant big extra bucks for my newly married, twenty-three-year-old self. My husband and I had been sleeping on a mattress on the floor in our bedroom for six months at that point in time. Maybe working two and a half months in the summer could help us buy an actual bed with a frame. I filled out the application to work both sessions, knowing we could really use the money and it would help to prepare me for the coming fall. I could have my room set up early and everything would be prepared. This included a few weeks of completed lesson plans, having folders labeled, educational posters hung up, and learning centers organized. BOOM!

When the end of the year came, I found myself to be completely wiped out. It was exhausting teaching, especially the first few years. I was desperately needing to take a break and recharge my battery pack, but I couldn't—summer school training started two days after Memorial Day. I knew the extra money was going to be awesome, but considering how drained I was, I began to deeply regret my choice to teach through the summer. Despite my bitterness, I pressed onward with the plan– I figured it was time to suck it up and bring home the bacon!

By the end of the second session of summer school, I did indeed have my room set up for the upcoming school year. I had most of my prepping done for what I would need in August and September and my lesson plans written for the first two weeks. What I didn't have was time to regroup, time to take a break so I could start fresh with my next group of students, time to enjoy one of the biggest perks of being an educator— SUMMER BREAK!

The class of kindergartners I was assigned my second year was the hardest group I ever had, both emotionally and academically. Some years are just like that. It would have been extremely beneficial for me to have allowed myself the summer to regroup so I could have the strength and energy I sorely needed to cope with the many challenges I was faced with during that immensely trying school year.

Procedures:

1. Take time throughout the year to refocus on why you became a teacher. Find ways to relieve stress (working out, talking to a good friend, meditating—whatever works for you!)

2. Remember that taking a break in the summer can help you to become a more effective teacher in the fall. I'm not saying you should never teach summer school. Just make sure that you are prepared, both mentally and physically, for the demands of teaching year round.

3. Take care of yourself. When you are flying in an airplane, there's a reason the flight attendants warn you to secure your own oxygen mask first before helping anyone else with theirs. How are you going to give your students oxygen if you can't breathe yourself?

Closing:

My September paycheck came and I was $2,000 richer. That money quickly vanished when I paid for a much-needed new car and took care of some bills. My husband and I didn't end up buying a bed. In the end, you could argue that the main thing I had to show for working the summer sessions was a painful start to the new school year, stress, anxiety, and an inability to be the teacher I knew I could and should be for my students. Eventually, I was able to get the ship on course and have a good year, but starts don't come much rougher than the beginning of that school year was for me. The point is, money comes and goes, but making time for your own emotional well-being is worth sleeping on a mattress on the floor and then some.

Reflection Questions:

1. Reflect upon what you enjoy most about teaching. How do these enjoyable moments make you feel?

2. List what you enjoy doing that helps you to recharge your battery.

3. How can you incorporate strategies to help you relieve stress in your everyday life?

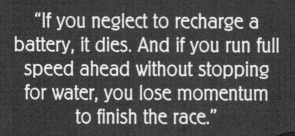

"If you neglect to recharge a battery, it dies. And if you run full speed ahead without stopping for water, you lose momentum to finish the race."

–Oprah Winfrey

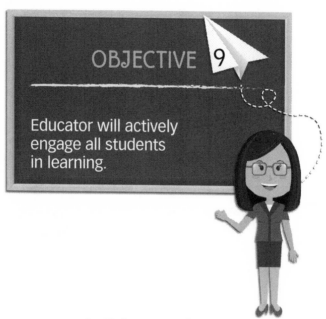

OBJECTIVE 9

Educator will actively
engage all students
in learning.

Anticipatory Set:

The Project Approach

For my student teaching placement, I had won the teaching jackpot. I was placed with an extremely experienced and bold kindergarten teacher in a school that was directly across the street from my house. This woman had been teaching for twenty-five plus years and knew exactly what she was doing. She was not afraid to stand up to policy makers; she loved her job as a teacher; the families at the school adored her, and she was well-known throughout the district. I learned more in my twelve-week student teaching experience than I had in all my undergraduate course work. Like I said—student teaching jackpot.

While student teaching, I learned various key components of education that stuck with me throughout my career as an educator. I witnessed the true value in student play while learning and how you need to allow ample time for their play. Center time was at least an hour on somedays, and the centers were set up intentionally to guide and promote students to use higher-order thinking skills. I learned how to build a classroom community by building meaningful relationships with my students. Being silly, laughing, and enjoying what was happening in the classroom were all present components of this kindergarten room.

I learned how to treat a paraprofessional as an equal and respected member of the classroom. These people are being paid much less than they are worth. If you are lucky enough to have a teacher's aide or paraprofessional, you know that they are the backbone of your classroom, and my student teaching experience showcased that! Most importantly, while student teaching I learned how to meet all learners in my classroom by implementing a style of teaching known as The Project Approach.

The Project Approach promotes students to actively participate in their learning through inquiry and student autonomy. The students choose what they want to learn about, develop questions for their topic, and find many ways to answer those questions. It meets the needs of children with all learning styles. I learned to teach with songs, texts, movement, hands-on experiments, and using outside resources to meet the needs of all of the many kinds of learners in my classroom. This type of teaching is more than having a thematic unit, which is what is often seen in Early Childhood classrooms. It goes beyond. The way my cooperating teacher used The Project Approach was through purposefully integrating the topic across content areas. For example, if the students were studying about the solar system, there would be a math lesson on making patterns with constellations and a language arts sequencing lesson on planets. The entire classroom would be transformed into a solar system with work the kids had made, song posters hung at student eye-level, and anchor charts with the students' questions on what they wanted to learn more about. She even had life-size student astronauts floating from the ceiling.

Learning this approach to teaching changed me! I began using The Project Approach immediately my first year. I believe in the value that allowing your students so much autonomy has in your classroom. Integrating subjects is a must, and allowing students to be inquirers of their learning naturally allows for catering to the many types of learners. I am so thankful I was placed in that student teaching experience. It shaped me as an Early Childhood teacher. In fact, I fell in love so much with The Project Approach that I used it as my thesis topic for my Master's Degree.

Procedures:

1. Allow your students the opportunity to choose what they want to learn about. I know many curriculums are already decided for you as a teacher, but you still have the flexibility to promote student autonomy by allowing them to develop questions they have about a topic and find ways to answer those questions.

2. Promote continuity across content by integrating curriculum in all subjects. If you are studying a unit on the history of the Gold Rush, implement lessons with all things Gold Rush! Use pretend gold to demonstrate place value during math, sing songs about the Gold Rush, talk about why the Gold Rush happened, and have students act out how they think people behaved, turn part of your classroom into an area where students can pan for fake gold.

3. Cater to all learners in your classroom. Not everyone can learn by sitting and listening to a lecture. Some students need to move, act, write, question, build, or see it on a poster. Do it all!

4. Use interesting materials during your lessons and actively engage students' interests through purposefully asking higher-order questions. Set the bar high. Even our youngest learners can benefit from using metacognition or being promoted to think about their thinking.

Closing:

Actively engaging all students in learning is a must. To reach the most kids you do need to go above and beyond. You absolutely cannot simply follow the basal text to reach everyone in your room. I highly recommend using at least parts of The Project Approach when teaching. I am not going to lie, it does initially take a bit more time to teach this way, but the end result is so worth it! I know that at the end of our Rainforest Project every year, I had five-year-olds who could name all the layers of the forest and knew which animals lived there. They understood the water cycle, how trees make the oxygen we breathe, and why conservation is important. None of this was provided in any teacher's guide I was provided. This type of learning came from within—developed from their natural curiosity about the world around them, fostering my students to want to be life-long learners. Isn't that what it's all about? Isn't that why we wanted to become teachers?

Reflection Questions:

1. How are you intentionally providing interesting materials for your students to promote learning?

2. How are you catering your lessons to impact multiple learners?

3. How are you actively engaging students in their learning?

"All learners can learn and succeed, but not on the same day in the same way."

– William G. Spady

OBJECTIVE 10

Educator will give students a voice in the classroom.

Anticipatory Set:

Crisscross Applesauce
and Shut the Hell Up

"SHHHHHHHH!" "Give me 5." "When my mouth is talking, your ears are listening." "Check your bodies." "Show me good body basics." "Crisscross applesauce and put your hands in your lap." These are all phrases that could be heard from my classroom all too frequently three to four years into my teaching career.

When I first began teaching, my students moved around on the carpet. They could fidget and sit on their knees if they wanted. They often called out answers to questions and added insight to read-alouds without raising their hands. I gave them choices in what we would learn about in science and social studies. Inquiry-based learning was my jam. Center time was long and meaningful—I actually played with my students during center time. I remembered and implemented the value of play in teaching. I made anecdotal notes about what my students were doing and learning. My creativity as an educator was flowing as a newbie. I remember those years as being very challenging, but more so, I remember them being extremely rewarding and fun.

I began to notice that not all educators thought my hippie-dippy, developmentally appropriate style of teaching was so great. Many comments were made by specialists, art teachers, librarians, music teachers, substitutes, and others about how my class did not know how to sit quietly on the carpet. Many made comments that all we did in kindergarten was play. "Oh, how easy to teach kindergarten. I wish *we* could just play all day." Unfortunately, I began to take to heart what others were saying about my teaching style. I started to gradually change as a classroom teacher and became more rigid with my expectations. I definitely did not want to be viewed as a bad teacher, and because of that, I began to go along with the herd. I began setting expectations for five-year-olds that seemed unnatural.

If you've ever spent any significant amount of time with a five-year-old, you know that sitting still and quiet for long periods of time is not one of their strengths. They like to wiggle, move, talk, laugh, ask questions, and share personal stories. My classroom started to become "The Teacher Show." At "The Teacher Show," the teacher does the talking. The teacher decides what we will learn about and where we are allowed to play. The teacher decides how you should sit on the carpet and when you are allowed to share your thoughts and feelings. The teacher worries about following the district guidelines of how many minutes should be spent with reading, writing, math, centers, and everything else. Needless to say, no one is having fun at "The Teacher Show." The school system really needs to cancel that show. It's bad television that produces terrible ratings.

Procedures:

1. Allow students to be autonomous in your classroom—give them opportunities for choice and leadership roles. Follow the students' lead in what they would like to learn about. Encourage inquiry-based learning by allowing students to choose some of their curriculum. After you know their interests, integrate ALL subject matters into this curriculum. If students find a spider outside, and want to learn more about spiders, follow their lead. Implement spider-themed math activities, research spiders online, develop questions as a class about spiders and find the answers. Live and breathe spiders!

I know many will argue that you are not given the freedom as an educator to follow the lead of your students because of district- or state-mandated curriculum. This is a sad truth. I get it.

However, I believe there are ways that you can connect students' interests to those requirements instilled from above. I strongly encourage you to not lose your freedom as a creative educator. This requires strength to push back, but the positive student outcomes you will see from allowing them some ownership of their learning is worth it.

2. Allow flexibility in your classroom. Does it really matter if all students are not sitting perfectly on the carpet with their hands in their lap at all times? Is it disrupting learning for students to sit on their knees? In my opinion, the trend of "crisscross applesauce and hands in your lap" is one of the worst things that has happened to Early Childhood classrooms. What an unnatural expectation for educators to have of their young students! I am not suggesting that you don't have any classroom expectations. Expectations are the backbone of the classroom. They keep everything aligned, but please make sure

that you consider how appropriate your expectations are for the age of children you are working with.

3. For the love of Pete, let the kids talk and share. Allow plenty of time for meaningful academic and social conversations. It's scary how little students are allowed to talk during the school day. Even lunch time can sometimes be a time of silence. This trend needs to end. A dear friend of mine was having trouble with her son when he began kindergarten. He was constantly coming home with a color change in his folder, indicating he had a bad day. She would punish him and take privileges away at home. One day, my friend asked her precious six-year-old what was going on. "Why are you having so much trouble in school every day?" "Mom, she won't let me talk," he spewed. "It's so hard, Mom. I don't get to talk all day!" It's a sad truth that many educators feel so much pressure to complete all of the demands of assessments and

curriculum that they don't allow time for student expression. This is a big mistake that's having a major effect on our children's emotional, social, and academic well-being.

Closing:

Giving students a voice in the classroom is one of the best things you can do as a teacher. This means allowing them choices in their learning, following their lead, building a community of learners, and allowing time to truly listen to their thoughts, ideas, and needs. I take full responsibility for the changes in student flexibility I made as a teacher. Looking back, it shouldn't have mattered what other educators thought. I wish I would have stuck to my instincts and knowledge of developmentally appropriate practices. There was one constant throughout my career as an educator—I loved my students and they loved me. That never changed.

Reflection Questions:

1. How can you allow student autonomy in your classroom to promote student ownership of learning?

2. How are you encouraging and promoting students being vocal in your classroom and preventing your class from airing "The Teacher Show"?

3. Reflect upon your classroom expectations. Are they appropriate for the age level of your students?

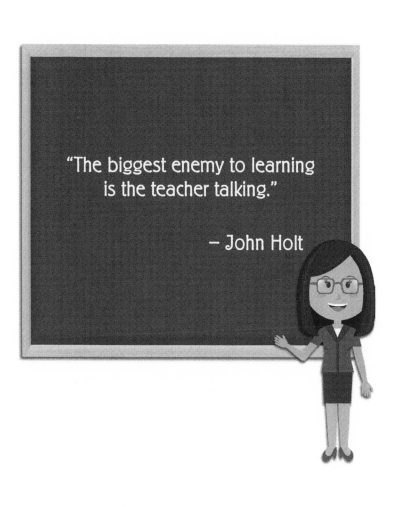

A YEAR IN REVIEW

I am by no means an expert on teaching. This book was written as a reflection of my time in the classroom. Hindsight is 20/20. I hope that one day I will be able to implement these lessons again upon my return to teaching, and I sincerely hope you can find value in these lessons as you go through your own journey as an educator. Reflect upon your enjoyment in the teaching experience, stay positive, roll with the many punches of education, be empathetic to students and families, be a student advocate, and (maybe most importantly) take care of yourself by recharging your battery.

I also implore you to take some time to be introspective while you are in the heart of your journey. As an educator, you will experience highs and lows. The pendulum of education will swing from one side to the other. Stay true to what you know is right about teaching and be an advocate for your students.

Happy Growing!
Colleen

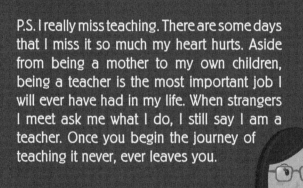

P.S. I really miss teaching. There are some days that I miss it so much my heart hurts. Aside from being a mother to my own children, being a teacher is the most important job I will ever have had in my life. When strangers I meet ask me what I do, I still say I am a teacher. Once you begin the journey of teaching it never, ever leaves you.

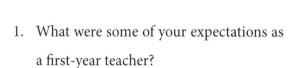

30 REFLECTIVE QUESTIONS FOR EDUCATORS

Here are all the reflective questions in one handy section.

1. What were some of your expectations as a first-year teacher?

2. How did you handle going with the flow when things didn't go as planned?

3. What strategies have you learned to better react to roadblocks that you may encounter in education?

4. How do you think learning the language of your students could impact student learning?

5. How could learning your students' native languages impact your relationship with students and their families?

6. What are some small steps you could take in order to learn a new language?

7. How does it make you feel when you see a teacher yelling at or humiliating a student?

8. What can you personally do to stop negative teacher behavior that is happening in your school?

9. If **YOU** are the educator who is behaving negatively towards students, what can you do to stop this behavior? Who do you have in your life that you feel safe enough with to ask for help in guiding you to change **YOUR** behavior?

10. How are you being an advocate for what you know is best for your students?

11. How are you an advocate for yourself as a teacher?

12. Reflect upon some of your best moments in the classroom. Was testing involved? Why or why not?

13. How can you genuinely show your students you care for them as individuals?

14. What are some ways you boost class morale in a large group setting?

15. Reflect upon times in your classroom when you shared smiles, laughter, and social conversations with your students. How do you think that positive environment impacted learning?

16. How do you think parents' past school experiences impact their relationships with you?

17. How would you feel about what is happening in your classroom if you were the parent of a child in your class?

18. How can you help to foster a partnership with your students' parents to become co-teachers in their child's education?

19. In what ways can you collaborate positively with your peers?

20. When and if you encounter school drama while teaching, what can you do to avoid it?

21. Make a list of educators you feel are positive examples of teachers. What qualities do they have that you could learn from to help you to be a better teacher?

22. Reflect upon what you enjoy most about teaching. How do these enjoyable moments make you feel?

23. List what you enjoy doing that helps you to recharge your battery.

24. How can you incorporate strategies to help you relieve stress in your everyday life?

25. How are you intentionally providing interesting materials for your students to promote learning?

26. How are you catering your lessons to impact multiple learners?

27. How are you actively engaging students in their learning?

28. How can you allow student autonomy in your classroom to promote student ownership of learning?

29. How are you encouraging and promoting students being vocal in your classroom and preventing your class from airing "The Teacher Show"?

30. Reflect upon your classroom expectations. Are they appropriate for the age level of your students?

Colleen Schmit was born in Omaha, Nebraska, and is the mother of three (soon to be four) children. Colleen began her career as an educator of young children in the Omaha Public Schools. She earned her master's degree in early childhood education at Concordia University in Seward, Nebraska. Colleen currently works as a bilingual program evaluator at the Munroe-Meyer Institute at the University of Nebraska Medical Center and is a part-time pre-K CLASS trainer through Teachstone. Colleen and her husband Bob enjoy spending time playing with their kiddos and eating lots of pizza.

ACKNOWLEDGMENTS

Writing this book was a big jump for me. It was a roller coaster of emotions that I wouldn't have been able to handle without a lot of compassionate folks in my life.

First, I would like to thank my incredibly supportive husband, Bob. Without his encouragement and unquestioning support I would have never made the leap into even thinking about doing something like this. His reassurance means more to me than he'll ever know. I love you, Bob!

There were many professionals that influenced my rookie years as a teacher:

Buffie Somers, my influential cooperating teacher for my student teaching placement. I experienced more from being with Buffie for twelve weeks than I could ever have learned in an undergraduate classroom. Her spunk and dedication to her students shaped my years in the classroom greatly.

Bob Acamo, my bold first principal whose passion about education was an inspiration to me.

Nicole Goodman, from whom I have learned so much about how to serve the needs of my students and their families.

Jonathan Wright, my patient and amazing Spanish mentor.

Last, but not least, my sister from another mister, Nicole Buchholz. Nic, you are the wind beneath my chola wings. Your friendship and encouragement every step of the way shaped this book.

I would also like to thank Teresa Hamilton, author of *It's Okay: Let's Get Real About This*

Thing Called Parenting. Thank you for your support and eagle-eye expertise when I first began this project.

Thank you to all of the influential women and professionals I have met while working as a program evaluator at the University of Nebraska Medical Center. Evaluation Domination is a team I am proud to be part of. I have never experienced such a wonderful work atmosphere filled with teamwork and sisterhood.

I would like to thank MK Mueller, author of *8 to Great: The Powerful Process of Positive Change.* Thank you for being an inspirational mentor and source of positivity and encouragement. I am so gr8ful for you, MK!

Thank you to Robert Pianta and the Teachstone Team. The CLASS tool has changed my views of education forever. A lot of my reflections on my time in the classroom were a result of learning the CLASS.

A special thank you to the amazing team at Concierge Marketing and Publishing. Lisa, Ellie, Rachel, and Sarah, I would have been a fish out of water without your guidance, creativity, and expertise.

Finally I would like to thank my fearless dad, Kevin, who told me, "If something doesn't scare you a little, it's not worth doing."

BRING
CRISSCROSS
APPLESAUCE

TO YOUR SCHOOL.

INVITE COLLEEN TO SPEAK TO
YOUR STAFF: 402-884-5995

SHARE YOUR FAVORITE MOMENTS
AS A TEACHER ON MY WEBSITE

www.CrisscrossApplesauceBook.com

85161689R00081

Made in the USA
Columbia, SC
18 December 2017